The Violin Close Up

The Violin Close Up

text and photographs by

PETER SCHAAF

FOUR WINDS PRESS   NEW YORK

LIBRARY OF CONGRESS CATALOGING IN PUBLICATION DATA

Schaaf, Peter.
  The violin close up.

  Summary: A close-up look at the violin, naming and illustrating
its parts and describing how it makes music.
  1. Violin—Juvenile literature. [1. Violin]
I. Title
ML3930.A2S23   787'.1   79-6337   ISBN 0-590-07655-8

PUBLISHED BY FOUR WINDS PRESS
A DIVISION OF SCHOLASTIC MAGAZINES, INC., NEW YORK, N.Y.
COPYRIGHT © 1980 BY PETER SCHAAF
ALL RIGHTS RESERVED
PRINTED IN THE UNITED STATES OF AMERICA
LIBRARY OF CONGRESS CATALOG CARD NUMBER: 79-6337
1 2 3 4 5 84 83 82 81 80

to M.B.G.S.

A violinist looks at the strings
and plays on them
with fingers and bow.

The bridge carries the music

down to the belly,

and the belly vibrates,

filling the air with sound.

The button anchors the tailpiece,

and stretch above the fingerboard,

where the violinist can play them.

An f-hole is cut

on each side of the belly,

and the sound flows around them

throughout the wood.

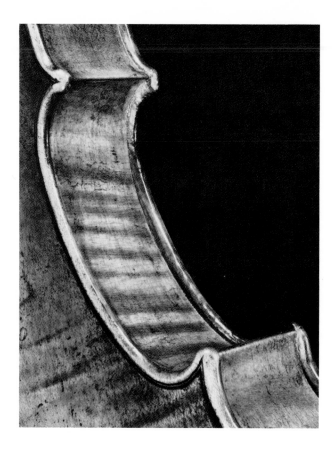

The corners, the ribs,

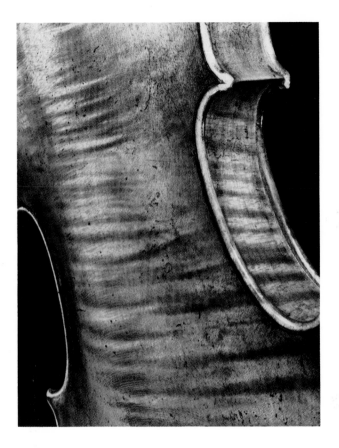

the waist, and the back

form a box under the belly.

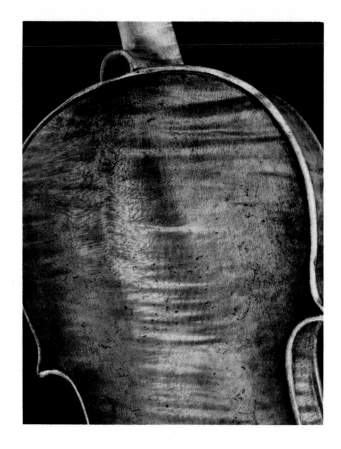

The shape of the box

makes the tone loud and beautiful.

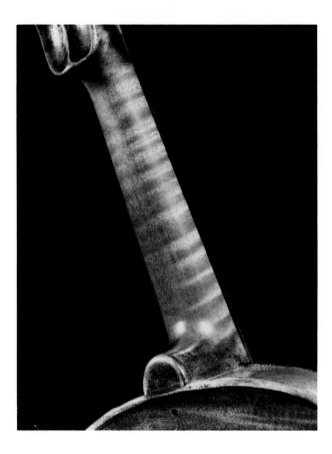

The neck supports the fingerboard,

and leads to the head.

When the strings reach the head,

they are pulled over the nut

and into the peg box,

where they can be tuned by the pegs.

The head ends in a beautiful scroll.

One hand holds the violin,
the other holds the bow.

_____

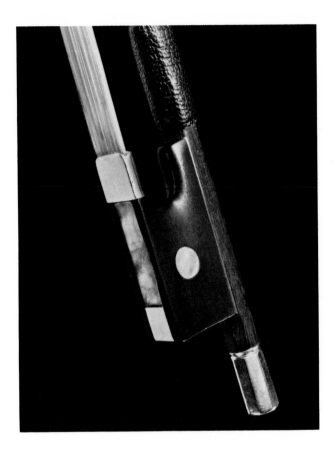

Hair is stretched tight along the stick,

from the frog—

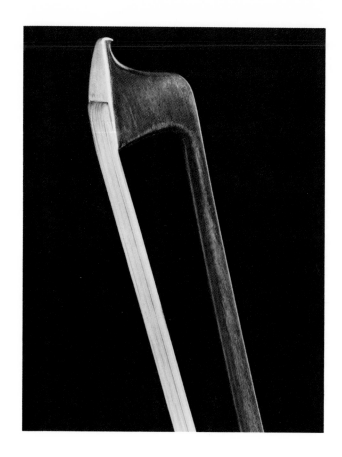

to the tip.

The hair scrapes the strings

to make music.

A NOTE ON THE PHOTOGRAPHY:

All photographs of the violin were made with a Sinar view camera and a 121mm Schneider lens. Polaroid 57 film was used for tests, and final exposures were made on Royal-X film rated at ASA 500. Exposure times ranged from 45 seconds to 45 minutes at a usual aperture of f64. Photographs of Mr. Kantorow and Mr. Christian were made with a Leica camera on 35mm Tri-X film.

Violinist on frontispiece: Jean-Jacques Kantorow, Paris, France.
Violinist on last page: Thomas Christian, Vienna, Austria.

Book design by Lucy Martin Bitzer.
Printed in duotone by Pearl, Pressman, Liberty Inc., Philadelphia.